3142
Lyndale
Ave. So.
APT. 2
PROSE POEMS
By Keith Gunderson
{20 ☮ SELECTIONS}

ISBN 0-913894-04-4

PRODUCED AND DISTRIBUTED BY

MINNESOTA WRITERS' PUBLISHING HOUSE
21 RIDGE ROAD
MORRIS, MINNESOTA 56267

for

Janice
&
Judy
&
Nancy

(cover by Christopher Gunderson)

BIOGRAPHICAL NOTE

Keith Gunderson has contributed poems to *Epoch*, *Chelsea*, *The Massachussetts Review*, *Western Humanities Review*, *Prairie Schooner*, *Burning Water*, *Trace*, *American Poetry Review*, *The Lions Tales* and *Eyes*, et al., and has had reviews of poetry published in *Chelsea*, *Kayak*, *Burning Water*, et al. He has published one previous book of poetry *A Continual Interest in the Sun and Sea* (Abelard-Schuman, 1971), and one of philosophy *Mentality and Machines* (Doubleday Anchor Books, 1971), and is the editor of the forthcoming *Language, Mind, and Knowledge—Vol. VII*, Minnesota Studies in the Philosophy of Science.

He is currently a Professor of Philosophy at the University of Minnesota, and a Research Associate in the Minnesota Center for the Philosophy of Science. He received a National Endowment for the Arts Creative Writing Fellowship for Poetry for 1974-75.

PREFACE

The contents of this book as well as its title belong to a sequence of roughly 150 poems which I eventually hope to publish in a single volume. Between 15 and 20 poems not included here are scheduled to appear in an anthology of prose and poetry edited by Chester Anderson to be called *Growing Up in Minnesota* and published by the University of Minnesota Press.

For the final shape and content these poems have taken I owe debts of gratitude to the following people, whether they like it or not: Robert Bly and Denise Levertov for having looked at some poems I had written in the middle 1960's. Both suggested (quite independently of each other) that my line-breaks were screwed up and that I needed to be composing with a much longer line. I took their advice and found that some of the things I wanted to say were best expressed in a prose-poem form. Such compositional strategies carried over to the poems presented here. The other two people I am most indebted to are my dear friend Alvaro Cardona-Hine and someone I know not at all, W.C. Bondarenko. I tend to see what I am attempting in this series of poems as being roughly equivalent to what Cardona-Hine was doing in his extraordinary (and extraordinarily neglected) book of prose sequences *Agapito* (Scribners, 1969)* which dealt with his boyhood in Costa Rica. My debt to Bondarenko stems from three wonderfully funny pieces ("Candy", "Pencil", and "Banana") about his own childhood which I read long ago in an issue of *The Minnesota Review* (Vol. IV, No. 2, Winter 1964).

Literary blather aside, the primary cause of these poems, for good or ill, was the incessant probings of my two sons Jonathan and Christopher (the cover designer) into "What was it like when you were a kid, Dad?"

K. G.
Minneapolis
January 1974

*It is hard to know the extent to which this neglect was enhanced by the soppy off-putting subtitle the publisher saw fit to stick on the dustjacket: "The poignant tale of a boy's unfolding world".

AN EPISTOLARY INTRODUCTION
by
Mel Jacobson*

(Fellow Alumnus, Jefferson Junior High, 1950)

Dear Keith,

I always thought you were lucky to live right by Bryant Square, and not have to run to the A & P, but could just run downstairs even in stocking-feet in cold weather to buy $.25 worth of lunch meat and a quart of milk at the basement store of 3142 Lyndale. But best of all you lived on the same block as Margie Benson. She went to Salem Lutheran with Marge Nelson and Sharlene (who actually married me) and Marlene. You went to Aldrich Presbyterian, but there weren't any cute girls who were Presbyterian. Still it's lucky you were Presbyterian so you could play for the church team at Aldrich when you got cut from the West High squad. You liked playing for God.

I suppose I can vouch for most of the stuff written in these poems. Jack and Ronnie and your dizzy sisters, even Janice, do exist. And you really were, as some of the poems suggest, a sort of chickenshit little kid. I still remember when you didn't like pulling a sweater over your head, though you were about 15.

One thing I have to admit, though, is that I coveted your fly rod. It's the one you must have been using when you went on those fishing jaunts to Lake Calhoun that you mention in "Grape Flavored Ice Cream Sodas". I remember your line going swoosha swoosha right out to those crappie and sunnie beds. I could never cast my 50 lb. test on my Langley rod and reel much more than 15 feet with a daredevil spoon. And I never hooked any big northerns around where you were catching all those crappies and sunnies. Sometimes I wished you'd step off a drop-off, or sink into one of those "quicksand" beds you talk about in *"The Girl of the Limberlost* and Homemade Quicksand".

I still find it hard to accept the fact that my childhood fishing pal and captain of the West High cross country team writes poems. But I'll bet that if our old English teacher Sig Stoylen read these he'd now be willing to recommend that you go to College.

With love from your big buddy,

Mel

*Mel Jacobson is a stoneware potter in Hopkins. He also teaches Art at Eisenhower High School in Hopkins, Minnesota. He has recently returned from a long stay in Japan where he studied in Kyoto with the master potter, Uchida.

MILK

I drank milk out of a bottle with a nipple on it until I was more than three years old and that's the only way I would drink milk because I fell in love with my bottle and nipple and even when there wasn't any milk in it I would carry it around like other kids carried their pacifiers and blankets and once I lost my bottle and nipple in a big snowbank during a storm and my Dad made loud words at me but walked carefully back and forth through the storm until he found my bottle and nipple and I was never without them at my side but one day when I was happy just sucking in milk my nipple fell off the bottle and milk attacked my face and made me scream and choke and cry and that was the end of milk for me no more milk never again you could never know what it was going to do to you and I didn't blame my bottle or nipple and still liked them but I never forgave milk and when I got to kindergarten I had a little speech defect because if I said wolf or roof or woof it always sounded like woof and woof and woof so one day each week I would go to a special class and work on my r's and l's and w's and was starting to get them right so they almost sounded different from each other but one day the special class speech teacher announced at us that the first one who worked out his problem would be awarded A GREAT BIG GLASS OF ICE COLD MILK which made me very scared because I'd almost worked out my problem which meant A GREAT BIG GLASS OF ICE COLD MILK would be coming at me soon so I went back to woof and woof and woof and the special class speech teacher said I should listen more closely because I had been doing very well but I had been listening more closely and could tell when someone was in cahoots with milk.

MY BARE FEET

When my Mom still had to dress me I was afraid of my bare
feet and if by mistake I'd get a look at them I'd yell MY
FEET MY FEET PUT ON MY SOCKS PUT ON MY SOCKS
and jump up and down trying to get loose from them but the
more I'd jump the more they'd seem to be part of me so my
Mom would tell me to stop yelling and jumping around and
sit still and she'd try to put my socks on me so I'd stop
yelling and jumping around and sit still except for jiggling
inside and stare at the ceiling where I'd be certain to see none
of my feet and wait and wait twice until a sock had captured
each foot and I was safe again and I was also safe when my
feet were inside the two foot-parts of pajamas with feet in
them and it was just great if my feet were inside socks inside
shoes inside overshoes but I was also out of danger if they
weren't inside anything at all but just under water in the
bathtub because though you could see them you knew you
could keep them under water if they tried to get funny and
my Mom used to ask me why I was afraid of my feet and I
didn't know what to say but I kind of thought to myself that
maybe I was afraid of them because when I first got a real
good look at them they seemed to be wiggling around by
themselves and even though they were me I wasn't sure they
were since they were the furthest things on my body away
from the rest of me and were like two strange animals I could
never run away from and I was never afraid of anyone else's
feet but only my own two though after awhile I just couldn't
worry about them either because there was lots else to be
scared of like quicksand and black widow spiders and funnel-
shaped clouds so my feet began to seem kind of friendly and
when I was still afraid of them my sister Janice would brag
about her feet and how beautiful they were and take them
out of her socks and smile at them but after I got so afraid of
other things and couldn't worry about my feet at all I'd let
my Mom make the littlest toes go wee wee wee all the way
home right before my eyes and my feet turned out to be
more beautiful than Janice's which were not bad as shapes
though they were really sort of flat.

SWEATERS THAT GO ON OVER YOUR HEAD

When I was four I got a sweater for Christmas that was blue and itchy and one of those sweaters that go on over your head and I'd never liked sweaters like that because before your head gets punched through the headhole you're in a dark place for a little too long so you start to think it'll never be light again and this new sweater which was my Aunt Molly's fault was the worst one of all because it had an extra-small headhole like it was made for a grapefruit sized head so after my Dad stuffed my arms through the sleeves and lifted the dark inside part of the sweater over my head and everything went black he began to smash my head through the headhole but I could tell by the feeling on the top of my head that it'd never make it so I started backing out but even my own Mom tried to block my escape and my sister Janice yelled about how she could help hold me but they wouldn't let her and then someone jerked the sweater back hard over my head until my head went through the headhole to just above my eyes where it stuck so I jumped and twisted and got away from everyone's grabbings and ran blind and screaming around the living room and tripped over my sister's new doll and fell down yelling and crying and my sister was shouting about her dumb doll that tripped me so my Dad and Mom finally joined my side and attacked the sweater and freed me from it and told my Aunt Molly who'd been waiting to see it on me that I'd try it on later and it sure would look cute but I wouldn't even put a dangerous sweater like that in my present-pile and stuck it over by Janice's doll and my Aunt said to my Dad whose other name was Luverne LUVERNE YOU SHOULD'VE JUST YANKED IT OVER HIS HEAD AND HE'D GOTTEN USED TO IT and I heard her say that and didn't want her to baby sit with me anymore and during the next few years there came to be a special drawer in my dresser set aside for those sweaters I got for Christmas and birthdays that were supposed to go on over my head but never did and I wondered how they liked being stuffed in a dark place with no way out.

HOW I LEARNED TO PEE STANDING UP

I was almost six years old before I learned how to pee standing up and the way I learned was once when I was going to pee sitting down my Dad walked in because he had to pee too and he said get up and let me show you how to pee standing up so I got up and he stood there not taking his pants down and peed standing up so I pulled up my pants and peed standing up and he said see how easy it is and I said yup and after that when I only had to pee I peed standing up.

THE BOXING CHAMPIONSHIP

When I was six years old I decided I wanted to box in a boxing ring and feel like a boxing champion but I didn't want to get in any real fights with kids my age because I knew they could all beat the pulp out of me I just wanted to do something that would make me be a boxing champion to myself so I thought it would be best to box my sister Janice in a boxing ring because even though she was five years older I wasn't afraid of her since she was only my sister but I knew she'd never do it even if I begged her so I figured out a way to trick her into it and got lots of string and strung the string around the chairs in the living room so that when Janice came home and walked into the living room she would walk right into my boxing ring and then I'd pop out from behind a chair with my swimming suit and mittens on and say DING DING ROUND ONE HAS STARTED and punch her in the stomach and make her cry and then hold up my own arm and dance around the ring yelling THE WINNER AND WORLD CHAMPION but when Janice came home she didn't walk into the ring at all but just hollered MOM KEITH'S PUT STRING ALL OVER THE LIVING ROOM YOU CAN'T EVEN WALK IN THERE MAKE HIM TAKE IT DOWN and went in the kitchen to get a glass of milk so I ducked into the bedroom and got her two favorite dolls and tied them up with leftover string to the legs of a chair so it looked like they were being burned at the stake and made a war whoop and shouted BURN HER DOLLS BURN HER DOLLS so Janice ran in and when she saw her dolls she screamed HE'S GOT MY DOLLS HE'S TIED UP MY DOLLS and went to save them so I popped out from behind the chair with my swimming suit and mittens on and said DING DING ROUND ONE HAS STARTED but before I could punch her in the stomach my mean sister smashed me right in the face with her hand and made me fall down and I screamed and cried but wouldn't hold up her arm and yell THE WINNER AND WORLD CHAMPION.

THE LITTLE KING

Sometimes me and Janice just before we'd fall asleep wouldn't fight at all because we'd do THE LITTLE KING on the bedroom wall and the way we'd do THE LITTLE KING was to get a teeny Coca Cola bottle about one finger long that any kid could get for free once a year at the Southside Picnic in Powderhorn Park and make the baby coke bottle stick to a finger by drinking the coke and then sucking the air out and smacking a finger right on the hole part of the top of it and waggling our coke bottle fingers around in front of lamps by our bed so the lamps would shoot shadows of the coke bottles on the wall and the shadows were fatter and bigger than the real coke bottles and were shaped like THE LITTLE KING who was a fat guy in a king suit in a comic strip and he never said anything or did much and was shaped like the shadow of a little coke bottle and me and Janice would make our LITTLE KING shadows walk all over the walls and ceiling and sometimes across our covers and faces and once even across my butt and we would try to say whatever we thought THE LITTLE KING might say and it wasn't hard because in the comic strip THE LITTLE KING never said anything so we could make our LITTLE KINGS say and do whatever we wanted and it was like running a whole comic strip by ourselves which had two LITTLE KINGS in it and when I got older and could read I didn't like THE LITTLE KING comic strip at all but I still liked to think of playing THE LITTLE KING with Janice and thought our shadow comic strip had been much better than the real one and even so good it was almost a movie.

INDELIBLE PENCILS AND ALLIGATOR SKIN

Once when I happened to be sucking on the end of my indelible pencil my sister Janice walked by and said you're going to get alligator skin so I asked her what alligator skin was and why I was going to get it and she said if you put indelible pencils in your mouth a lot pretty soon hard slimy green scales will grow over your whole body and even your face except for the eyes and you end up looking just like an alligator so I asked her how much you had to suck your indelible pencil before the scales would come and she said I'd probably sucked mine enough already since she'd seen me do it yesterday and the day before that but I could see she was trying to make me cry so I held it in but I asked my Mom if she thought I'd turn into an alligator and she said she'd certainly be surprised and gave me a funny little smile that made me feel better but Janice shouted LOOK AT HIS TONGUE MOM LOOK AT HIS TONGUE IT'S ALL PURPLE. ICK. HE ALWAYS SUCKS ON THAT PENCIL HE'S GOING TO GET ALL SCALY HE REALLY WILL so I snuck off to the bathroom and got a washcloth to wash off my purple tongue just to be on the safe side and rubbed until my tongue was a very light blue that no one would notice but Janice noticed it right away and said YOUR TONGUE'S STILL BLUE so I went back and scrubbed some more and took a good look at a scab I had to make sure it was where I'd scraped my knee on the sidewalk and not the start of any alligator skin and then I took off all my clothes and checked around myself to make sure the rest of me was o.k. and it was so I went off to find Jack and when I found him I asked if he knew what alligator skin for people was and he said sure that's what you get if you eat indelible pencils so I told him how I'd been sucking on mine for a few days but he said he was sure that wasn't enough because you had to chew up all the indelible stuff in a lot of pencils and be a baby or a real

7

little kid before the scales would come because after you got to be nine or ten your system could fight off alligator skin and his brother knew a guy who knew someone whose kid had gotten into a box of indelible pencils and chewed up three or four and the scales came almost right away and they didn't know what to do because there's no cure for it so they rented the kid out to a circus as a freak so he'd be able to make a living when he grew up because there's nothing else you can do with skin like that and he'd always have to spend at least ten hours a day in a tub of water or he'd die and I felt sorry for that kid but better for myself after talking with Jack because I knew Jack knew more about alligator skin than Janice so I went home to tell her what a dope she was and that you couldn't get scales by just sucking a bit on indelible pencils at my age but what I wanted to do most was buy an alligator suit and sneak it on at night after she was asleep and let her find me in the morning next to an almost empty box of indelible pencils but I didn't have any money to buy a suit like that so I just cut up an old billfold and pasted a few pieces of it on my arm but it didn't look much like alligator skin so I never tried the arm out on Janice.

STURDY AND SPARKLE

And because tooth-health which was also called dental hygiene was one of the most important things you could learn about in Grade School there was a special lady who popped in on our class at Lyndale Grade School a couple of times each year to emphasize teeth and how they could rot in your mouth but she knew you might not be too excited about it anyway so she brought along two puppets she had to stick her hands in to make move and she croaked out a little frog voice for the boy puppet and a little screechy high-up voice for the girl puppet and she hoped the puppets would help make it fun for us to think about our mouths and how our teeth would all fall out pretty soon if we didn't brush them up and down and up and down the right way and she told us the puppets were brother and sister so no one would joke about how they horsed around with each other the way Stanley and Patricia did and they each wore blue and white sailor suits sort of clothes with a big red bow pinned to them and had mouths with very white non-rotting teeth in them which grinned all the time and the brother puppet was named Sturdy and the sister puppet was named Sparkle and the special lady who had complete power over what they'd say about teeth would always start them out in a sort of stage of a house so it looked like it was going to be a story or play the puppets were in so it always started out o.k. with the little house being by the sea or deep in the woods or on top of a mountain and we would be made to think some great adventure was just around the corner but after a minute or two Sturdy and Sparkle would find some reason to be brushing their teeth together and one of them would be doing it right and the other would be doing it wrong and the right brusher would be telling the wrong brusher why he or she was wrong or was forgetting to massage gums or was drinking too much sugary pop and not enough bone-building milk and after watching Sturdy and Sparkle brushing away for a couple of years lots of us would make "oh no" sounds when we were told that today we were going to have a couple of little visitors in to talk with us about dental hygiene but the teachers never even heard those sounds but when I'd go home from the special lady and Sturdy and Sparkle I'd brush my teeth fast every-crazy-which-way and never up and down and up and down like Sturdy and Sparkle did because once I tried doing it their way and felt just like a great big brother puppet in a blue and white sailor suit with a red bow and someone's hand inside my back and fingers up my arms making me brush that way and I would rather feel like a kind of criminal than feel like that.

9

THE VICTORY GARDEN

We were told that one of the ways we could beat the Krauts and the Japs and bring peace and brotherhood to all the world again was to grow a Victory Garden which was a little garden your whole family would take care of in order to grow food to eat so you wouldn't have to buy so much store food so the food that would have gone to the store would be sent to feed Our Boys Overseas and the other Allied Forces so they'd be strong in battle and smash through to victory on all fronts so we rented a little plot of land out in Bloomington for a Victory Garden and the main thing I tried to do to help beat Hitler and Tojo was to plant a corn seed in a flower pot at home so that after it got too big for the pot I could take it out to our Victory Garden and plant it there and I did and tied string to some sticks I'd stuck in the ground all around it so it wouldn't get lost or stepped on and I couldn't wait for my corn stalk to get as high as my Dad and have ears of corn so I could pick them and have my Mom cook them up and put butter and salt on them and munch corn against Hitler and Tojo while Our Boys Overseas and the other Allied Forces munched on the corn that my Mom would have bought at the store for me but a big dog or cow or maybe my sister didn't look where they were going and knocked down the string and sticks and crushed my corn stalk so I never got to eat any corn from it but we won the war anyway.

It was in Miss Bechter's 5th Grade class at Lyndale Grade School that we were all commanded to learn a poem by heart and be ready to recite it the next day in front of everyone and some of us remembered to learn a poem but most of us didn't but Ronnie Robertson saved the day for a few of us at least for a little while because when it was his turn to recite he just said something he'd known forever which went TEN LITTLE PIGGIES ON THE MOUNTAIN TOP / COME LITTLE PIGGIES AND EAT YOUR SLOP and sat down and folded his hands and looked straight ahead and nobody giggled out loud and Miss Bechter went right down the row to the next one who was Carol Nelson who snapped up straight and said TREES BY JOYCE KILMER and then said the whole dumb poem without a mistake though she went too fast but when she tried to zip by the part about the tree being pressed to the earth's sweet flowing breast some of us whisper-giggled and Bob Esser said a bit too loud that he'd like to see a tree growing out of a tit which made Miss Bechter say TIME TO GROW UP TIME TO GROW UP REMEMBER BOYS *SOME* OF YOU ARE GOING TO BE 6TH GRADERS SOON SHALL WE GET BACK TO BUSI-. NESS but as soon as we got back to business a girl tried to get away with TWAS THE NIGHT BEFORE CHRISTMAS WHEN but that's all she got out before Miss Bechter said that wasn't the sort of poem she had in mind and that the girl had better look for a different poem and try again tomorrow and then it was Jerry Beckley's turn which made everybody wonder what he'd try to get away with this time and this time he just yelled TEN LITTLE PIGGIES ON THE MOUNTAIN TOP / COME LITTLE PIGGIES AND EAT YOUR SLOP and grinned at Ronnie Robertson but Miss Bechter interrupted his grin by saying *Mr.* Beckley was supposed to stand when he recited so Mr. Beckley jumped up and yelled it again and Miss Bechter let it go by because it was Jerry and because she'd just been cross about TWAS THE NIGHT BEFORE CHRISTMAS but pretty soon she was also cross about the piggies poem because when the next guy tried it she made a noise with her foot and said THAT WILL BE THAT which we all knew meant no more about the piggies and we were on our own but Earl Kinard who was a kind of daredevil and didn't care too much about his future and getting into the 6th Grade didn't give up right away and when it was his turn to recite he gambled on *NINE* LITTLE PIGGIES ON THE MOUNTAIN TOP / COME LITTLE PIGGIES AND EAT YOUR SLOP and won and ended up in the 6th Grade.

SPITTING

I was the only one who could beat him at checkers but whenever we had spitting contests Paul Donahue would win over me and everyone else because he practiced a lot and had the right sort of hole between his front teeth and could work up a special kind of spit without any spray to it and he was so good at spitting far no one ever came close to spitting spit near his and it was like he wasn't spitting at all but shooting a mushy bullet out of his mouth of a gun and he was famous all over the neighborhood and sometimes we'd ask for his recipe and although he would tell it to us we could never make spit like his in our own mouths so we knew he must have been born with a special sort of throat and tongue and teeth and we'd never be able to beat him so sometimes we'd sneak off without him in order to have exciting spitting contests of our own where we wouldn't know at the start who'd end up the winner and when my 4th Grade teacher Miss Bergstrom explained to us that the real word for spitting was to expectorate and that IF YOU EXPECT TO RATE DON'T EXPECTORATE I knew she didn't know nothing about how good and famous Paul Donahue was at to expectorate and that even if I told her she wouldn't believe me.

GRAPE FLAVORED ICE CREAM SODAS

Once when my Dad and me were coming back from crappie fishing in Lake Calhoun without any crappies we stopped at SNYDER'S DRUGS for a treat and the treat I got was a grape flavored ice cream soda and it was really good and even so good I asked my Dad to taste it a little and he did and then snuck another taste and said it was really good and the next time we came back from crappie fishing in Lake Calhoun without any crappies and stopped at SNYDER'S for a treat we both got grape flavored ice cream sodas and told each other how really *really* good they were and a few weeks later when it was hot and everyone was sitting around the apartment melting my Dad asked me if I felt like having one of those grape flavored ice cream sodas and I said I did feel like that and thought that him and me would be walking up to SNYDER'S without Janice but instead my Dad had decided to make grape flavored ice cream sodas all by himself for the whole family and said if you think those up at SNYDER'S are good wait'll you taste mine I could show that soda jerk a thing or two your old man almost went·into the restaurant business you know and I knew he sort of almost had because he loved to say he almost had but I was surprised about the grape flavored ice cream sodas because I'd never seen him make one or even heard him talk about them before I'd had one at SNYDER'S but he said he made great ones and if I'd get my nose out of my comic and run down to the basement store and charge twelve bottles of grape pop and a quart and a half of vanilla ice cream we'd all have as much as we wanted and my Mom asked my Dad about just how much he thought we wanted but he didn't even hear her and I yelled I wanted three or four giant sodas and Janice said she wanted a root beer float instead because she didn't like grape but my Dad said no root beer float could hold a candle to his grape flavored ice cream sodas so I ran down to the store and got six bottles of grape and the ice cream and then I ran down again and got six more and when I got back upstairs I saw my Dad had already poured the first bottles in the Thanksgiving Turkey Roasting Pan and had begun to stab apart all the ice cream with a knife and smash at it with a big wooden spoon and then he poured in the rest of the pop and began to stir the ice cream around and around until everything began to look purply white and kept smashing away at any ice cream lumps he'd spot bobbing around in the pop and none of them escaped and pretty soon it all looked kind of soapy and you didn't see what you'd see if you looked in your soda at SNYDER'S and my Mom asked my Dad if he was sure he knew what he was doing but he said she had to be kidding and kept stirring and stirring and then said ALL RIGHT GET DOWN THE GLASSES and poured the funny looking stuff into the glasses and gurgled his own down in a couple of gulps and announced THAT'S BETTER THAN SNYDER'S YOU CAN BET YOUR BOOTS ON THAT and my Mom took a little sip of hers and said she'd never had one of them before and it certainly was different and I tasted mine and yelled IT'S TOO WARM AND THERE AREN'T ANY HUNKS OF ICE CREAM LEFT and my Dad said that's the secret of my recipe it's much smoother than any soda you can buy in a drug store so I almost began to cry but remembered I had my own nickle and ran down to the store and bought a vanilla ice cream cone and plopped the scoop into my soda and Janice said she thought it looked icky and didn't want any but my Dad kept on drinking the stuff until he said we could save the rest for later and it'd keep and if we wanted it colder he'd make it colder and turned the refrigerator way up and yanked out a lot of jars and plates of stuff so he could get the rest of his secret recipe in but he had to pour it into three smaller bowls because the pan wouldn't fit and my Mom made popcorn and we all went into the living room to listen to THE SHADOW on the radio while my Dad's secret recipe sat in the bowls and the next morning me and Janice went to look at the bowls and there was just a lot of scummy stuff on the top of each one and purply white pop underneath so we laughed and laughed because Dad had already gone to work and I asked my Mom if she'd like some purple swamp for breakfast and in the afternoon I caught my Mom pouring the three swamps down the sink and when she saw me see her she said I don't think Dad will miss this very much and when Dad came home and looked in the refrigerator he said I see you've finished it off afterall and my Mom said we sure did Dad we sure did.

THE GIRL OF THE LIMBERLOST
AND HOMEMADE QUICKSAND

I first learned about quicksand because Janice my old sister
was reading a book called THE GIRL OF THE LIMBER-
LOST and in the book the Girl of the Limberlost's boyfriend
or father or cousin or someone dies by sinking in quicksand
and that put the jeebies in me it was just another scare to add
to black widow spiders and funnel-shaped clouds so I asked
my Mom about what quicksand was and she said it was lots
of sand mixed with lots of water and too thick to swim in
but thin enough to sink quick in and to be careful when
walking by lakes and not to go near swamps and I didn't say
anything about our Apartment Building at 3142 Lyndale
Ave. So. being built on an old swamp and that Jack had told
me it was settling a bit more every year and that some year it
would just disappear which almost made me want to move
but I thought a lot about quicksand and would look carefully
at sand near Lake Calhoun where I liked to go swimming and
sometimes I'd first find a stick and push it at patches of sand
which looked a little bit different though I would have just
run carelessly over them before Janice told me about THE
GIRL OF THE LIMBERLOST but I never found any sand
that acted like quicksand and I really wanted to and wanted
to capture some in a bottle and take it home and watch it
work but since my Mom said it was just sand mixed with
water I thought I could make some myself and not get hurt if
I was careful and went down to the sandbox in Bryant Square
and filled up a big paper bag with sand and carried it back to
3142 and climbed up in the cupboard and got down the big
yellow bowl my Dad always made his world famous Tom &
Jerry's in at Christmas and I started running water in the
bowl and tested the bowl with my arm which was skinny and
the bowl seemed too deep and maybe with quicksand in there
I'd end up with my arm getting stuck so I got down a littler
bowl which I knew I could jerk my arm back out of no
matter how quick the quicksand was and after I filled up the
bowl with water and dumped in the sand I sat for a while just
looking at it and wondering if I'd made quicksand and how it
would work and finally I shoved my arm in the bowl way up
to my elbow and tried to just let the sand grab it down but I

couldn't tell if I'd let my arm go or not because letting your arm go isn't like dropping something since you're always sort of there in your arm and then I cheated and pushed the arm down and squished it into the sand and a lot of water ran over the sides of the bowl onto the floor and then I decided the arm was too big and that I'd pretend the two fingers next to a thumb were a walking man and tried to let him try to walk over the sand and then be grabbed by it but the fingers didn't work any better than the whole arm and didn't sink down like the guy in THE GIRL OF THE LIMBERLOST and then I didn't even believe I'd made quicksand though when my Mom came in and asked about the mess I didn't confess I'd tried to make quicksand because I knew she loved me and would have been mad at me for ever having taken such a chance.

MY TAPEWORM

After I got to be nine or ten I started to eat a lot for lunch and dinner and in-between and big snacks before bed but I still stayed skinnier than any kid on the block even Allen Burke so my sister Janice decided I had a tapeworm and she made the announcement about my tapeworm at dinner one Sunday after I'd had three helpings of mashed potatoes and gravy and the extra drumstick she'd wanted herself and said KEITH'S GOT A TAPEWORM. I'M SURE OF IT. and went on to say it was probably a great big one because I ate so much and stayed skinny and was even skinnier than Allen Burke and if there wasn't a tapeworm in me to help out I'd be fat as a pig and someday she was going to get a piece of raw liver and hold me down and force my mouth open and dangle the liver which all tapeworms love right above my mouth and when my tapeworm stuck his head out of my mouth to grab the liver she'd grab him and pull him right out every foot of him but I didn't even cry one bit because I knew she was jealous of me for eating the extra drumstick and thought liver was real icky to touch and screamed like crazy when I three little angleworms at her.

THE WOMAN WHO SWALLOWED AN OCTOPUS EGG

And my friend Jack's brother knew a guy who knew someone who was related to a guy who was married to a woman
who was standing on a beach by the ocean one day when a
wave with an octopus egg splashed in her face while she was
talking and made her swallow the egg though she didn't even
feel it going down but later on she got very fat and went to a
doctor and the doctor announced that she was going to have
a baby and when she felt she was going to have it her
husband drove her to the hospital but when they operated on
her they didn't pull out a baby person at all but a perfect
looking octopus about the size of a football except for the
arms and one of the nurses fainted and a doctor almost threw
up and it was such a terrible surprise the doctors and nurses
didn't want to tell the mother of the octopus about it because she'd die of shock and they didn't even want to tell the
father but one of the doctors decided the father should know
and went out to talk to him and worked up to the octopus
by asking him if his wife had been near an ocean during the
last nine months and when the guy said she had the doctor
explained about the danger of swallowing waves and how
parts of some waves might have octopus eggs in them and
then he broke it to the guy that that's what had happened to
his wife and that their baby was really an octopus but he
took it pretty well and donated the octopus to an aquarium
without saying how it was born because he didn't want any
publicity and he never told his wife or anyone except the guy
who told the guy who told Jack's brother who told Jack who
told me and the woman who had the octopus lived and went
on to have five human children of her own.

THE NEW BABY

And when the new baby came I was already nine years old
and too grown up to be jealous of her or even care that I
wasn't the youngest one in the family anymore though I
didn't understand why my Mom didn't just have the baby in
the hospital and leave it there for the doctors and nurses to
take care of for a little while and pick it up later so she'd be
able to come home and make lunch and dinner for the rest of
us as usual instead of ditching us and letting it be up to Dad
and Janice to take care of me for almost a whole week and
my Dad brought home lots of chow mein from the Nanking
and that was good but once it was left up to Janice to make
me dinner and all she made me was lunch which was Camp-
bell's Chicken Noodle Soup which was pretty good but the
rest of it was a peanut butter and jelly sandwich that was
terrible because it was two things I liked crushed together
into one thing I couldn't stand but I kept my chin up and
made it through the week and when my Mom finally showed
up with the new baby she flashed it around the whole apartment building and I felt completely invisible whenever I was
with her and my new little sister named Judy because even if
I stood right next to my Mom all the people did was to gawk
at Judy and maybe finally ask me how I liked my new baby
sister but even when I said I just loved her they didn't listen
but kept gawking at the baby and making funny sounds in its
face and once I thought if anyone asks me how I like my new
sister I'll say I think she stinks but I didn't because I knew
my Mom would hear it and then maybe my Dad would hear
what she heard and that could mean THE SLIPPER even
though my Dad said I was too big for it now so I just went on
saying I loved the baby and a few days after the baby started
living with us my Mom said I could hold her if I sat down in
the big chair so I did and said how darling and cute and little
she was and that I'd told Jack I'd build model airplanes with
him so would someone take the baby off me and ran out the
door and yelled I'd play with the baby later though I couldn't
think how a dumb baby could play anything but after awhile
I figured out some things to play with her and one I called
tickle-pinchy which we played when my Mom gave her a bath
and I'd tickle her to make her laugh but if she didn't laugh I'd
say tickle-pinchy and do a harder sort of tickle just to

19

make sure she could feel it and sometimes my Mom would interrupt and say not so hard Keith she's still pretty little and after she got to be not pretty little Jack and me would take her out in the stroller by ourselves and one of the best games we did was to race her and pretend it was The Indianapolis 500 and sometimes I'd get her going fast down a hill at Bryant Square and Jack would catch her and there was only one teeny crash during all the times we played Indianapolis 500 and even when I got to be thirteen I still liked playing with her and the best game I played with her then was Mop which was hiding in the clothes closet with Mel Jacobson with an old gray mop and calling for Judy and then making the mop pop out of the clothes like a monster which would make Judy scream and run to my Mom and make me and Mel laugh and laugh at the good joke we'd played on my beautiful little sister.

A SURE DIAGNOSIS

(for John Daniel)
And when I was about ten years old I started reading THE
READER'S DIGEST every time it showed up and first I'd
read about the most unforgettable character someone had
ever met and then I'd read the jokes in the part called Life in
these United States and then I'd read about whatever disease
was the special one for that issue and once the special disease
was all sorts of V.D. but mostly Syphillis and how you could
get Syphillis through sexual contacts and how most of the
people who got it were too embarrassed to go see a doctor
until it was too late and their body had begun to rot and the
germs had smashed through to their brains and made them
crazy and afterwards it would murder them and I asked Jack
about sexual contacts and Syphillis and he said you could get
it by putting your dink in a girl who had gotten screwed by a
guy who liked to screw sheep but you also could have sexual
contacts with toilet seats that were public like the ones down
at Bryant Square or at Nicollet Ball Park or even by just lying
in the grass with your swimming suit on where someone with
Syphillis had been and left germs which could jump down
your suit even if you tied the strings tight and a few weeks
after I read about Syphillis I was taking a pee and noticed
that my dink hurt so I looked at it and it was a little bit red
and sick looking so I knew I'd had some sort of sexual contact
and gotten Syphillis and that if I didn't get to the hospital
soon my body would rot and I'd go crazy and die but I was
embarrassed about it just like the article said everyone was so
I didn't dare break the news to my Mom and when Dad came
home I was too embarrassed to tell him I'd had sexual contact
and gotten Syphillis but I started to sweat and be nervous and
snuck off to the bathroom to pee again to see if it still hurt
and it did and my dink didn't look right so I yelled for my
Dad to come in and I quick shut the door and showed him
my dink and said it burns when I pee I wonder what's wrong
with it and didn't let on about the Syphillis but my Dad took
only a quick look at it and said it's a little irritation of some
sort but be sure to wash yourself good when you take your
bath so I said I guessed it wasn't any big disease and he said he
was sure it wasn't so I said it's probably not V.D. or Syphillis
or anything like that and he said he was sure it wasn't anything like that and I said I was sure it wasn't anything like
that.

21

THE APPLAUSE-O-METER IN THE BATHTUB

When I got to Jefferson Junior High School I started falling in love with even more girls than I'd fallen in love with at Lyndale Grade School and not only Joanie Nelson but also Corky who was really Cecille Pearson and Patty Gooler and Sharon Devereux and one would be my girl friend for a little while and I'd be happy but then I'd be ditched for some older guy and Sharon Devereux ditched me for about four older guys all at once and one was already in the Navy and sometimes I'd even be given up for someone my own age and be told that we could always be friends and I couldn't figure it out but I'd feel terrible for almost a week or two and would start taking lots of extra baths because when I took a bath I could pretend I was a terrific singer on some talent show because when I sang in the bathtub my voice sounded pretty good and not like it really was so I'd sing my head off and feel sorry for myself but get revenge on my ex-girl friend by being the underdog on the talent show but turning out to be the best singer to come along since Frank Sinatra and Vaughn Monroe and the way I'd work out the talent show in my head in the tub was to have it my turn to perform and nobody knowing who I was and Dick Contino and his accordian being No. 1 on The Applause-O-Meter so I'd come on stage and sing some great song like TENDERLY or I'LL SEE YOU AGAIN or BLUE MOON and the whole audience would go crazy and clap so hard I'd beat Dick Contino and by accident the girl friend who'd just ditched me would be in the audience and be proud of me and in love with me again because I was on my way up the ladder of show business but she'd be sad since she knew I might not take her back and would be kind of crying at my beautiful singing and sitting next to her new boy friend she'd ditched me for who couldn't sing any better than a frog and finally she'd rush backstage to congratulate me and show me she wanted me back and then it would almost be the end of my bath and sometimes I'd take her back but sometimes I wouldn't and would just walk away from her in my own head and wait until the next night to take her back when I took another bath and turned out once again to be No. 1 on The Applause-O-Meter.

NAMING THE STATE BIRD

And because we lived in a democracy all the school kids got to vote for some bird to be The State Bird and in fact any kid in any class in any grade except kindergarten could nominate a candidate for The State Bird and after the voting the results would be sent to the guys who had been elected to run The State of Minnesota and they would figure out democratically which bird was the lucky winner and I guess the wood duck was or the loon but no one who was in our class which was 8th Grade Room 205 at Jefferson Junior High had ever even heard or thought about those birds so they didn't get considered and there were six or seven of us who were boys who played a lot of ball together and got in trouble for fun so the bird we nominated our class to nominate was THE CHICKEN and anyone in favor of a particular class nomination could give a speech on behalf of that bird so we all gave speeches on behalf of THE CHICKEN and talked about eggs and eating chicken on Sunday and what other bird did so much for everyone and one of us questioned a guy who'd come out for THE CARDINAL about what a cardinal could be used for and all he could think to say was that they were red and pretty and a baseball team was named after them so we booed and hissed at the cardinal until the teacher said no booing or hissing allowed and then the teacher remembered that although she wasn't permitted to vote THE ORIOLE was her favorite bird and probably quite a few people liked THE ORIOLE and they build such interesting nests so about two seconds later at least five kids really liked THE ORIOLE and nominated it even though one of them thought it was green but we kept talking up the usefulness of THE CHICKEN and when the votes were counted THE CHICKEN squeaked in the winner with THE ORIOLE second so we laughed and clapped until the teacher reminded us that laughers and clappers could stay after school and that democracy was a serious business and there'd be no more nonsense about messy chickens and since THE ORIOLE came in second and was the only SERIOUS candidate of the two it would be the nomination of Room 205 and one that we could all be proud of.

THE STRADIVARIUS IN THE LOCKER

Any family that had an apartment at 3142 Lyndale Ave. So. also had a locker in the basement where they could store all the junk they couldn't use and wouldn't throw away and in the big pile of junk in our locker I found a little brown violin with no strings and one crack and which looked sort of pretty when you wiped the dust off so I asked my Dad about it because he was a terrific piano player and almost became a piano teacher and knew everything about music and had studied music at The McPhail School of Music and he told me I should be careful when I fooled around with the violin because it might be a Strad . . . and then I couldn't understand what he'd said so I asked him what he'd said it might be so he said the same word again so I had to ask him again and then he said very slowly it might be a STRAD I VAR I US which he said was a violin made by the best violin maker in the history of the world and if we had one it would be worth a fortune and one of these days he'd take it down to Schmitt's Music store to see if it was a STRADIVARIUS which it probably was and he'd cash it in and we'd move out of this dump but my Mom said that if that violin was a Stradivarius our TV set was a CHIPPENDALE and I didn't ask her what she meant but my Dad asked her what SHE knew about it and she said she didn't know anything about violins but she knew a lot about Dad so then I knew what she'd meant and we both laughed and even Dad laughed too because he couldn't help it though at the end of his laugh he snuck in a little heh heh heh he could help and said that after he cashed the violin in he'd send her a postcard from the Bahama Islands where he'd be retiring and my Mom said I'll be waiting Dad I'll be waiting and don't forget to send last month's rent with the postcard and when he finally got around to checking out the violin it wasn't a Stradivarius or even a Chippendale but we'd moved out of the dump anyway but I'd loved 3142 Lyndale Ave. So. for such a long time I didn't know why my Dad had called it a dump anymore than I first knew what he meant when he called the violin a Stradivarius.